COLD MOON

TURTLE POINT PRESS *Brooklyn, New York*

COLD
MOON

*On Life, Love,
and Responsibility*

ROGER
ROSENBLATT

Requests for permissions to make copies of any part of the work should be
sent to: Turtle Point Press, 208 Java Street, Fifth Floor, Brooklyn, NY, 11222
info@turtlepointpress.com

Library of Congress Catalogue-in-Publication Data
Names: Rosenblatt, Roger, author.
Title: Cold moon : on life, love, and responsibility / by Roger Rosenblatt.
Identifiers: LCCN 2020030494 | ISBN 9781885983886 (hardback)
ISBN 9781885983893 (ebook)
Subjects: LCSH: Life. | Love. | Responsibility.
Classification: LCC BD431 .R557 2020 | DDC 814 /.54 —dc23
LC record available at https://lccn.loc.gov/2020030494

The author and publisher wish to express their gratitude to the following
parties for use of copyrighted material: for excerpts from "An Arundel
Tomb" by Philip Larkin: Farrar, Straus and Giroux; for excerpts from
"Pike" by Ted Hughes: Farrar, Straus and Giroux and Faber & Faber;
for excerpts from "August Moon" by Robert Penn Warren: William Morris
Endeavour Entertainment; for excerpts from "September Song" by Kurt
Weill and Maxwell Anderson: Warner Chappell and Hampshire House;
for excerpts from "We've Only Just Begun" by Roger Nichols and Paul
Williams: Hal Leonard; for excerpts from "Bird on the Wire" by Leonard
Cohen: Sony/ATV Songs; for excerpts from "Get Happy" by Harold Arlen
and Ted Koehler: S. A. Music; for excerpts from "I Got Rhythm"
by George Gershwin and Ira Gershwin: Warner Chappell Music Inc.

Design by Alban Fischer Design

Hardcover ISBN: 978-1-885983-88-6
Ebook ISBN: 978-1-885983-89-3

Printed in the United States of America
First Edition

Wipe the tears from your face, and see the boulevard of light the Moon has cast on the black water. See the boulevard as a staircase laid flat for a moment before it takes shape and rises, like the one in the movie *Stairway to Heaven*, a sort of celestial escalator made of white marble steps moving forever skyward. The story is about a courtroom trial in heaven, a battle for a man's soul—whether he should die young as he was scheduled to do or be allowed to remain on earth and live out a long life. A woman's love for him wins the case. Love wins the case.

Wipe the tears from your face, see the moonlight, and rise. No need for a stairway. Hold on to your soul. One shot of courage, and we're climbing.

✦

Sitting on the beach with my ten-year-old grandson, Sam, I watch his brother, six-year-old James, balance himself while standing barefoot on the top rail of a high white wooden fence. James does things like that, climbs something and finds a perch, disregarding any possible danger. Now, dressed in red shorts and a Washington Nationals blue T-shirt, he is gazing out to sea, his little body angled away from Sam and me.

"It's a wonder how James goes off on his own and takes in whatever he can," I remark to Sam.

Without turning to me, looking admiringly at his brother, Sam says matter-of-factly, "He loves life."

✦

Midnight on December 20, 2019, nearing the advent of the year of flawless hindsight. A bloodshot orange presents itself without notice on the northern horizon, just above the dark beach and the dark sea. This is the Cold Moon, also identified as the Long Night's Moon, the last before the winter solstice. My weathered mind flicks to my own winter solstice, the coming of my wintertime of life. Through a three-windowed wall, I watch and brood.

The sea rolls out like an old dog into its own black coat. The Cold Moon, now saffron-white, sketches a sporadically spotlit path, recalling the jungle runways I saw in Africa when I was a journalist, writing about wars. Dim lights, like phosphorescent animals, murmur at the far end of the beach, the beach itself a bench of robed jurists versed in maritime law. A solitary tern hangs in the air on the word "wait." An unseen magistrate asks, "Who is responsible for this wreck?"

How still is night. And with every passing year, a hardening of the arteries. The bones fray. The skin puckers. The skills ebb. At this age, comrade, at this stage, what is to be done? Should we toss in the towel? Or gallop across the Anichkov Bridge together, in the opposite direction from whence we came, and, like the czars, make a palace of winter? I am a book in your lap.

Better to know where to go than how to get there. I wander from thought to thought, having learned but three things from my Long Night's Moon: I believe in life. I believe in love. I believe we are responsible for each other.

✦

Blood roses; life; a golden bubble of the sun; a rhetoric of shadows; redeeming snow; life; the click of the lock; the crackpot; the camo kayak; the littered dock and mottled face of the kiosk; where is the drowned girl?; life; you are the reason the creek exists; you are the creek; I, on the other hand, am not myself; the other hand; life; a success of geese; blood orange; swallow your pride, yet one swallow does not make a summer; redeeming light; the annals of your eyes; blood on a boxing glove; blood on a tunic; well, did you ever; what a swell party this is; life; the departure of kings; down the hatch; down the thatched roof to the rocks; an Irish on the rocks or neat, or not; life; an ecstasy of daffodils; a parody of weeds; a comedy of eros; if you're ever in a jam, here I am; if you're ever in a jelly, rub my belly; life; let the brass section wail; bring on the oboes; the hobos too, in the dark terrain of Richard Wilbur; where is the drowned girl?; the bronze grip of fear; fear of the bronze grippe; playgrounds; coffee grounds on Stevens's "Sunday Morning"; they've clogged the drain; evidence of rain; ravens explode upward in a black parachute; life; a chipped swollen desk in a corner of a schoolroom; and lookee here, cloves; there will come a time for the drowned girl; there will come a time for her; life; a flattery of moonlight; redeeming moonlight; and the Cold Moon acknowledges the glitter of the sea as a day moth folds its wings and sings "Goodnight, Ladies"; it swings; moth dreams; rub your angry skin till it's raw; blood on your knuckles; blood on your thighs; cast your aspersions to the winds; your icons, bygones; frantic; pedantic; antic; Atlantic; life, life, life.

✦

One afternoon, I heard a thud from the kitchen. When I went to look, a dead bird lay on the deck outside the sliding glass door. The glass door had brought about the death of the bird, which must have mistaken it for open air in the blinding sunshine. The bird's body had left an imprint on the glass, vague and lacy, like a smoke ring from a cigarette. The imprint was a complete circle, except for a small smudge at the top, where the bird's head must have hit.

The little guy lay on its back on the deck, still as any sun worshipper. I did not recognize the markings. Green, orange, and brown, like a mallard but smaller. When I picked it up to put it in a ziplock bag, the bird felt heavier than I had anticipated. The body had heft and substance. Only when I had tossed it in the trash and returned to the house did I notice the imprint on the glass door. It was there that day and remained through the following morning and a few days after. I would wipe the glass door clean eventually but not that day. The smoke ring was all that was left of the bird.

✦

What will you leave behind?
This book and that.
What will you leave behind?
This gesture, that smile.
What will you leave behind?
A faint imprint, a feather.
What will you leave behind?

Would you please repeat the question?
What will you leave behind?
I don't know. Love?
That's more like it.

✦

Comets change course because of forces unseen. The earth's magnetic field determines the motions of the animals, us animals included. You can't see gravity. You can't see faith, emotions, wonder, love. Or good old God, of course. You can't see God. Just as well, probably. None of these forces is visible, yet who doubts their power? When you think of it, everything visible is controlled by something invisible. The visible Cold Moon. The visible sea. The visible you.

✦

The other night I watched *Bang the Drum Slowly* for the third time. Best baseball film ever. Leaves *Bull Durham* in the dust. Have you seen it? Michael Moriarty plays a star major-league pitcher, and Robert De Niro plays his catcher, a sweet-natured, none-too-bright country boy on whom his teammates rag relentlessly. Moriarty tells the story. We learn that De Niro is dying of Hodgkin's lymphoma. The team is hot, in the pennant race, and Moriarty hopes to keep his catcher in the lineup as long as he can, until the disease makes it impossible for De Niro to play. Privately, Moriarty negotiates a contract with the team's owners that says De Niro cannot be traded unless Moriarty is traded with him. He'll take less money, but that's the deal. Where De Niro goes, so will Moriarty. That essentially is what the film is about. One guy sticking with another.

In the run for the pennant, the De Niro character starts to hit better than he ever did. He is a solid singles hitter, so his teammates do not feel as though they are carrying him. But the lymphoma continues to eat away. Moriarty tries to keep De Niro's deterioration a secret from the manager and the other players, but eventually word gets out. None of his teammates treat De Niro with pity. Even the one sentimental moment in the film, when everyone gathers round a guitar in the locker room and sings "Streets of Laredo," is done without tears. Whatever the guys are feeling, they just play ball. At the end of the final game of the season, won by Moriarty, De Niro is weak and disoriented. He staggers helplessly around the plate. The last scene of the film shows Moriarty taking his friend to the airport for a flight home, to die.

In the end, Moriarty says of his catcher merely that he was a pretty good guy, no worse than most.

"And not a bad ballplayer neither, when they gave him a chance" and laid off teasing him. One thing Moriarty has learned: "From here on in, I rag nobody."

✦

Everybody grieves. That's the key to responsible mourning—remembering that everybody grieves. Philo said, "Be kind, for everyone you meet is carrying a great burden." In grief it is difficult to think of everyone, but when you do, beauty intrudes upon sorrow, and something lifts. Everybody grieves.

Some years ago, a finback whale washed up on this beach not far from where I am watching now. Finbacks, or fin whales, as they are sometimes called, are sleek and fast. They can race with steamships. Stretched out on the pebbles, the poor dead beast was enormous, nearly sixty feet long. The carcass was as tall as a cottage. Its tail was distinct, but its eyes were submerged under a veil of skin, beige like a woman's slip. The head was striped and was the size of a small car.

Round and round the animal everyone walked. Curiosity seekers, strangers to one another, they walked round the whale like a procession of monks, whispering and muttering. A few took notes. The moon snapped on like a ship's lamp, and the whale itself seemed lit from within, like a great porcelain globe of the world. Everybody grieves. We are responsible for each other.

✦

My mother is teaching me to read. I am two and a half. We sit together at the dinette table with a book between us. I remember nothing of the book, or of any of the others we read, but I can still feel her closeness, the fresh-flower smell of her clothing. From her early seventies until her death from Alzheimer's twenty years later, my mother will show only the look of fear. She will look anxious even in death. But when I am little and she is in her mid-thirties, my mother is the face of serene competence. She strides, arms open, into life.

We make eggnog. She teaches me to stir the eggs and pour in the vanilla. We sew on a button. We run the vacuum. We sweep, dust, do the dishes. We make beds. "Do you know that one is supposed to be able to bounce a quarter off a newly made bed?" she says, and laughs. "But who has a quarter!"

We go shopping in the neighborhood. People acknowledge her and wave. "Hi, Molly!" She buys a rose for each of us at the Gramercy Florist. She buys a baker's dozen of cupcakes at the Gramercy Bakery and explains that a baker's dozen means thirteen. She takes me with her to the neighborhood milliner on Twenty-Second Street. The shop is dead quiet and the proprietor snooty. "How do you like this one?" my mother asks me, deliberately tilting what looks like a brown stuffed owl over her eyes. I giggle. "We'll take a baker's dozen," she tells the milliner. He is unamused.

✦

A wave is created by a rolling cylinder of energy passing through particles of water that rise and fall vertically. When you're swimming in the ocean or are out in a boat, individual waves exist only relative to you. In terms of how close they are to you. The same is true of the wind. Whether windward or leeward, you pay attention to the wind as it affects you. This is to say: The wave is your wave. The wind is your wind.

Yet you know that isn't so. We share the world with one another—everything in it equally available to Kurt the barber in Bed-Stuy and his half sister Olga in Prague. It's hard to acknowledge you are part of a multitude. No? The imagination resists the idea of belonging to any group, much less to vast unseen populations. This may be why we do not get along in groups. Yet we will perish with the thought.

Right now a subway conductor in Tashkent is

remarking on the brightness of the Cold Moon. Do you hear her?

✦

A quick intake of breath, and I am in the dark again. In it, before it. This night is so loud with light, and yet I tend toward the darkness that contains nothing but itself. Not a scare, not the past, not my guilt or yours. Present yourself to it, though it has not called for your presence. It has nothing to do with you. Present yourself to it as one would to any fact of this world—a rose, a ship, the dark. There. It does not make a move toward you. It does not retreat from you. You do not expose it or enlarge or defeat or clarify it. It has nothing to do with you. Or if it does, it simply offers a test for you: To see the thing itself, for itself. To see the noun. Am I able to face into the dark without asking for help? Am I able to face you without asking for help? Do not help me.

✦

The sea's sounds change from gulps to sighs. I feel the cold wind slice through the windows and recall something about our mutable lives. All species are linked. The closer the connections, the more genetic information shared. I know this. How do I know this? Evolution's chains interacting with ecology's chains. A single species becomes every species.

How do I know this? Aspirin comes from the bark of a willow tree. Penicillin from a mold. One species heals another. What is to be found in the African sausage tree, or in the bark of a Pacific yew, or in the Madagascar periwinkle? A little clarity, if you please. I rise to greet the ocean, like a gentleman at the dinner table. Beyond, the Cold Moonlight messes with the water. "Killers from the egg," Ted Hughes called us, our species, in "Pike." Killers from the egg. Can nature die?

Astronomers have just discovered subtle boundaries on the surface of Mars, which they call the "fretted terrain." Poetry is fretted. Poetry hides in the mutable world. As the poem tells you what it wants you to know, life tells you what it wants you to know. Sing Hallelujah, come on get happy. Or be a writer and get shit-faced while playing stride piano in a Jersey dive. I am vague about specifics, but I know that the world is to be seen generously. I know this. How do I know this? At the village dump the other day, I watched four homeless men set fire to a pile of prosthetic legs for warmth—and s'mores. Hold me up to the Cold Moonlight. Look for the watermark.

✦

John Stuart Mill came home one night to discover that his housekeeper had tossed the massive manuscript of Thomas Carlyle's history of the French Revolution in the fireplace. Carlyle had given the manuscript to Mill to read. The housekeeper had thought it was wastepaper. Of course, Mill felt awful. But Carlyle did not chastise his friend, or weep, or wail, or feel sorry for himself. He simply sat down to write his history of the French Revolution all over again.

Life, you are my history of the French Revolution. Shall I write you again, from scratch? Or shall I scoop up the housekeeper's mistake and kiss the ashes? Make a history of the ashes? Give, sympathize, revise. The end of art is peace.

✦

J. B. Priestley's play *An Inspector Calls* opens with a wealthy English family celebrating the engagement of the daughter. The prospective marriage is a sound one in terms of the father's business interests, the upper class merging with the upper class. Cheerful noises and chatter all around. Glasses clinking like the bells of doom. But then an inspector calls, because a young woman, a dismissed factory worker, pregnant, has just killed herself by swallowing a bottle of disinfectant. And one by one the inspector traces the responsibility for her death to each member of the family. They did it, every one of them, directly or indirectly. They killed the pregnant girl. As he leaves, the inspector looks around the room and tells them, all lives are intertwined: "We don't live alone upon this earth. We are responsible for each other."

In the environs of Houston, a species of mimosa tree is infested with a particular species of beetles. The female beetle becomes pregnant and must lay her eggs. She crawls out on one of the older branches of the mimosa, partway to the end, and cuts a deep longitudinal incision in the bark—down to the living tissue of the branch. In that deep slit, she lays her eggs. Then she goes somewhere else. The eggs grow and crowd out the surrounding tissue of the branch. The branch dies and falls to the earth. Then and then only do the eggs hatch, and a new generation of beetles goes off to the other mimosa trees. Tree and beetle cannot get along without each other. The beetles prune the trees, which are said to be healthier and to live longer than any other trees in Texas. A predatory relationship thus gradually shifts to that of parties who agreed to get along. They are responsible for each other.

Among humans, not long after conception, the cells of the mother and of the child-to-be initiate a

two-way chat across the placenta. Microchimerism—
that's what it's called—begins a silent chemical trans-
action, a cellular communication between mother
and child that continues years after the child's birth.
The mother's fetal cells may be found in the child's
bloodstream and in the skin and in all the major
organs, including the heart. It is also thought that
the microchimeric cells increase the mother's toler-
ance for successive pregnancies, so that microchimerism represents an altruistic act of first children to
support the lives of their genetically similar sisters
and brothers. In the resulting evolutionary process,
shared cells may change who people are, may in fact
change the species. In that case, all we need in terms
of the improvement of the race is the mating of two
perfect people, and we're in like Flynn. Killers from
the egg? That Ted. What a caution. We are responsible for each other. Cellularly speaking.

✦

In the Crimean War, Florence Nightingale used to
patrol the hospital tents and set her hair on fire
to distract grievously wounded soldiers from their
agony. A legless kid, barely seventeen, is writhing
in his stumps on his cot, and Nurse Nightingale
reaches for her Zippo. Go with the Flo. She was
responsible for others. Nuts, but responsible.

Would it be too crazy to take my kayak out tonight? It's a sturdy little boat, built for oceans. A vessel testing human capability. When you're kayaking, you are wholly responsible for your decisions and your actions. You have the sensation of complete freedom, but you're only as free as the wind and water allow. The best part of the experience is how it heightens your senses. You are supremely alert, aware of everything, as one is on a ship. Only in a kayak, you pretty much are the ship.

Speaking of which, did you see the news about the derelict cargo vessel that crashed on the rocks off Ballycotton, on the southern coast of Ireland? Not a soul aboard. A ghost ship. It had come up the African coast, then farther north, west of the Spanish coast, then west of the English coast, and up to Ireland. On its own. A big mother, 250 feet, originally headed from Greece to Haiti when it became disabled. The crew was taken to Puerto Rico, where the ship was supposed to be towed to shore. But that never happened. The ship had been drifting ever since.

Things like that are not supposed to be. A ship with no one on it, sailing alone and empty, in storms, in calms, without human guidance. A victim of destiny, like the rest of us. If I went out and lost control of my vessel and drowned, would I leave a ghost kayak? Empty boats upon the ocean. I can feel that way. I am an empty boat upon the ocean, out of the cradle, endlessly rocking.

✦

Missing persons are not supposed to be. We cannot abide the idea. Someone is gone. Someone disappears and is never seen again. Unthinkable. The corpus cannot be tied to the delecti. The court needs evidence that a crime was committed. Even in the light of a confession. Even in the face of an eyewitnesses to a murder. A hundred eyewitnesses. A thousand. Two thousand eyes. We need to see the body. The kids' faces on milk cartons. A guess at how tall they would be, and of what weight, today.

Judge Crater. Jimmy Hoffa. Natalee Holloway in Aruba fifteen years ago, last seen at a nightclub. Where did she go? They all "pulled a Crater." We need to see the body. Where did Amelia Earhart go in the sky en route to Howland Island from Papua New Guinea? Missing in the sky. We look up and squint. Where are you, Amelia, with your smiling tomboy face, in your monoplane? Playing peekaboo behind the Cold Moon?

Come out, come out wherever you are—all of you missing persons. Absence, absence. A cry of absence in the heart, in the winter solstice of my heart. If you exist, we exist. If you do not exist . . . We long for evidence. We need to see the body. Your body, ours. Who's missing in the classroom? Who's missing in the army lineup? In the prison roll call? In the sky? In the nursery? The search, eternally futile. Where is the drowned girl? I miss you. Wish you were here.

✦

I doubt God every other day, yet I pray all the time. I pray without God. Prayer is the sound of longing. In the chapel of my longing, I pray.

✦

When we lament that we've lost our connection to nature, to the natural world, what does that mean, exactly? What are we missing? It has to do with the nature of nature, I think, which is stoic and steady. While I yearn and jump about, the sea out there is just out there. It goes about its business, its sea business, unaware of and uninterested in the frantic little boats that ride it. Why do we lament that we've lost our connection to the sea? Because the sea, for all its rock and roll and danger, knows itself, accepts itself, and that's its value. Nature fills the background of our lives with a self-reliant peace. What are we missing? Peace.

What should one make of these pictures—these landscape photographs of Oleg Ershov? He has been named International Landscape Photographer of the Year. He's more than that. A conjuror? A kayak? An egg?

This one, for instance, taken in a place called Fleswick Bay in England, of shades of Permian and Triassic sandstone, waterborne, two hundred million years old, in the shape of horizontal human legs, knees slightly raised, as if the people were stretched out facing one another. And in the groove between one of the pairs of legs, a gray egg of a rock. Killers from the egg? Possibly. Everything possibly.

Size and proportion are impossible to determine. The rock may be an oval softball or a boulder, the legs leg-size or minuscule or as enormous as river valleys, dry river valleys. "My passion for landscape photography," said Ershov, "is based on a love of nature, especially in places where human intervention is not yet visible." But the imagination makes human intervention visible everywhere. Our naked, pockmarked legs, with an egg among them. We constantly take the Rorschach test.

What then do I see in you? Other than you, I mean. I should see nothing in you other than you.

19

You should be enough for me, plenty. Yet the imagination ruffles the mind. You are the leg and the egg. You are Fleswick Bay, England. You are the shades of Permian and Triassic sandstone, waterborne, two hundred million years old—burnt umber, beaver, chestnut, chocolate, cocoa, and desert sand. You are everything, possibly. You are my love.

✦

Heraclitus was cute but full of it. You can never step into the same river twice? Sure you can. It's just that the river exists in a state of continuity, so what you step into is the motion that defines the river. But it's always the same river.

The point is that certain things are made of change, and the river is always true to the change that defines it. Life, too, is made of change. Thus the phrase, always said with a shrug, "that's life."

Of course, all this riddling chatter raises the question: What are you doing stepping into the river in the first place? What was Heraclitus doing? You can drown stepping into a river. Just sayin'.

✦

On a train long ago, in the "Coloreds" car, just ahead of the caboose, the Dixieland Five sleep in their burdensome woolen overcoats. The band is wiped after sixteen club dates in a row, in every Alabama small town from Camels to Chesterfield. In the aisle lie their instruments, also asleep—the bass and the horn and the trombone and licorice stick and the drums, all piled in a great slag hill, like possessions taken from prisoners. The train clacks and grumbles into the long silky night.

Asleep, the band looks like plans gone awry, as good as dead. But then the trombonist, Mikey "Brainy Boy" Arlen, who once was apprenticed to none other than Trummy Young, opens first one eye, then the other, leans into the aisle for his instrument, and starts in on the first few bars of Kid Ory's "Muskrat Ramble." And Kansas "Busboy" Lehrer reaches for his clarinet and joins in, followed at once by Garry "Lips of God" Trudeau on the cornet and Alan "Heebrew" Alda on the sax, with "Running" Ronnie Berman now thumping the bass and "Li'l" Bobbie Reeves plunking himself in the middle of the aisle and beating the hell out of his drums.

And all at once there's jazz on the train. And the people from the other cars—club car, dining car— white folks all, they sit up in their seats like puppies and follow the music toward where its coming from, snaking a conga line through the train until they reach the "Coloreds" car. And all of them, black folks and white, are singing that muskrat song, and slapping their palms against their thighs, and tapping their shoes, into the long silky night.

✦

And Oleg Grigoriyevitch Kuvaitsev, nicknamed Allegro, because he jumps and pops around like a runaway musical note—what of Allegro? He, too, plays sax, having built his own instrument as a kid growing up in Leningrad and listening to American jazz. He stuck a clarinet in a samovar, and it moaned like a sax. Later, he formed the Leningradski Dixieland Band and toured Sacramento, Milwaukee, and much of the Midwest, USA.

You want life? Allegro is life in a samovar—souped up, ten-steps-ahead-of-you life. Today, he leads me on a tour of his city, shout-singing as he goes: "I got rhythm, I got music, I got my band. Who could ask for anything more?"

We are heading toward Raskolnikov's house, the real house in which Dostoyevsky created a room for his fictional philosophical murderer. I am writing the *Time* magazine essay to accompany the photographic book *A Day in the Life of the Soviet Union*, one in a series of such books on a day in the life of various places. Rain paints the city in a blackened silver. I ask Allegro about the denial of freedoms for Russians, if it affects his music. "Freedom is like a girl," he says. "I love her. She does not love me." He skitters ahead. "But," he says, "are your American liberties unlimited?"

We come to the Anichkov Bridge, which he calls "the Bridge of Sixteen Balls." I ask him why. "The statues at either end," he says. "Four males on horseback, four male horses," he says. "See how much freedom your magazine gives you to print that!"

✦

Sisters and brothers, shall we join hands? At the dinner table, at the picnic table, at the pool table, at the water table; at High Mass, at Silent Meeting, on the High Holy Days, at the baptisms and bar mitzvahs, in the amen corner with the Pentecostal choir singing in tongues—wherever the congregation congregates, shall we join hands? Among the cries of the crazies and the swinging of the hammers and the flashes of pain, it's worth a shot. Don't you think? Remember what Brecht said when asked what we should sing about in the dark times. He said sing about the dark times. Loud, lusty singing. No cowering in a parenthesis. That's the ticket. The world's a buddy system. You have my back. I have your aorta. Who will start us off, sisters and brothers? Who will get the hymn going, hitting the keynote? Perfect pitch. With a tuning fork or a Jew's harp. A hush spreads over the welts of the ocean like a prayer, like a prayer shawl. Look, there in Antarctica, at the foot of the icebergs. Can you spot the dusky dolphins?

✦

Because this excursion of ours is unavoidable, to say nothing of perilous, should we not go for supplies? Like Tonto, I mean, when the Lone Ranger sent him on errands to the feedstore, for feed, or to the general store, for generals—to Bloomingdale's, say, to gather up all the essentials we'll need. Soap. Thread. Diamonds. That sort of thing.

Just the going was a cause for celebration, you said. The trip itself would be a trip. And I'll buy that. Yet should we not address the fact that during three or four days and nights in the desert, we will yearn for a good old hot dog stuffed with sauerkraut and all the fixin's and soda pop?

This excursion—it's about us, isn't it? It's about making our way over the fretted terrain of Mars to the weir, then down to the swimming hole, then up the flagpole, is it not? Will anyone salute us? Research shows that couples do better crawling around on full stomachs than spending a life of clucking and cavils. (Did I write that?)

Think of our going as a returning. The way heroes

return in the Greek epics. The way Odysseus goes round the Aegean before dropping in on Penelope again. So different from Western epics in which the heroes just go, go, go west. You and I come back. The circle may be vast, but we come back. Right? Please say I'm right.

Oh, hell. Forget the diamonds. Forget the supplies. Forget everything. No amount of preparation will equip us for each other. That's a fact, Jack. Let's just go. A kiss for luck, and we're on our way. We've only just begun. To live.

✦

Voices. How many do you have? A Jeanette MacDonald–Nelson Eddy duet? A barbershop quartet? The Hi-Lo's? The Mormon Tabernacle Choir? I hear your voices in the sea winds, under the fog, near the bow of my kayak. A buoy bell clangs. Red, right, returning.

✦

Then I ran out the front door and looked to the left and to the right, quite panicky and chicken-like, but you were nowhere in sight. Vanished, into thin air, like Orson Welles in *The Third Man* after he shows his face to his friend Joseph Cotten, who thought Welles dead. Welles runs. We hear his footsteps echo on

25

the wet Vienna cobblestones. Then there's no trace of him where the footsteps led and stopped cold, at the square with the cluttered kiosk.

And that was you. You disappeared like that. Your footsteps had stopped. And I looked all over, scoured the dark streets, quite panicky and chicken-like. And all I saw was a cluttered kiosk in an empty square.

But you're not a criminal. You didn't sell black-market, watered-down penicillin. You would never do a thing like that. You're you. Oh, you might snatch an apple from a street cart, possibly. Or jaywalk. Or tell me a lie or two. Or three. But basically, you're a good person, and I respect that.

Yet you disappeared in a puff of smoke. Without as much as a "beg your pardon," or a "by your leave," or a "how d'ye do?" I hardly know what to make of it. Where should I look for you? I've already scoured the sewers of Vienna. I even rented a zither, hoping you'd come out, come out wherever you were hiding once you heard the zither music. Our life isn't a movie, you know. I could live in postwar Vienna forever and never see you again. Is that what you want? Or will you show your canny face in the doorway once again, and stay put, while the light of the postwar Vienna evening kisses you chastely like the Cold Moon.

✦

The latest from Antarctica is that the world's biggest iceberg, the size of Delaware and Rhode Island, is breaking up and drifting out to the Southern Ocean. Who can blame it? It has to be a burden, being that big and solid. I couldn't do it, I'll tell you that. If I were the world's biggest iceberg, I, too, would want to chip away from myself and drift. I couldn't bear the pressure of all that colossal adamancy. The only thing I'm certain of is my uncertainty. Nope. Let me wander aimlessly into one sea or another. Chop me up into ice cubes and let me float in a vodka tonic. May I freshen your cocktail? I drift and fall apart too easily to maintain the size of Delaware, even Rhode Island.

✦

On TV, when I was a kid, I saw the demonstration of a toy, a kind of novelty gift. It was a wooden box, about a foot wide and six inches high and deep. The only things the box contained were an on-off switch and a little mechanical hand. When you turned on the box, the mechanical hand would rouse itself and turn the box off.

The perfect absurdist thing. No? Beckett could have invented that box. Or Sartre, or Kafka, or

Robert Musil. Maybe Musil more than the rest. The box existed to unexist itself.

Reminds you of the stones the gulag prisoners were forced to haul in wheelbarrows for many miles, day after day. The prisoners would dump the stones at some appointed destination and then go back for more to add to the pile that eventually became a minor mountain of stones. Many of the prisoners would survey the site and take a kind of pride in their accomplishment. At that point the gulag guards would order the prisoners to take the stones in the minor mountain they had created and wheel them back to their original location. This they did over and over.

More was at stake in the gulag projects than in my novelty box, surely. But the principle of doing something for the sole purpose of doing nothing is the same. So here is what one might say to the stone-hauling prisoners. Since the nature of your torment is not going to change, it is you who must change. Notice the stones. Cherish each stone.

And to the little mechanical hand of the self-defeating box? In the few-second interim from when the time on becomes off, why don't you learn to play the mandolin?

✦

In peace, Love tunes the shepherd's reed;
In war, he mounts the warrior's steed;
In halls, in gay attire is seen;
In hamlets, dances on the green.
Love rules the court, the camp, the grove,
And men below, and saints above;
For love is heaven, and heaven is love.
> —SIR WALTER SCOTT, from *Lay of the Last
> Minstrel*, quoted in *Stairway to Heaven*

✦

Have I told you about the time when I was three that my folks called the police to go find me? I wasn't lost, though they did not know it. I had simply gone wandering on the beach early one morning when my family was on vacation in Cape Cod. The sun was just up and pink, but the air was already hot. I wore a big straw hat, like the ones in Winslow Homer paintings, and a bright blue bathing suit. Nothing on my feet. Down the beach I walked, listening to the burble of the water on the shore and taking everything in. The carcass of a dead horseshoe crab bobbed in the damp sand. I picked it up and kept walking, swinging the black shell at my side.

How long I walked I cannot say. But after a while I heard the police car siren behind me. The red and blue beams of the car's lights created paths of color on the sand. I turned to see a policeman with my parents in the front seat. The car pulled up, the siren groaned down, and the three grown-ups trotted toward me. I just stood there smiling with my horseshoe crab.

"You can't just wander off without telling us," said my father.

"We were scared to death," said my mother.

I smiled some more and hugged them, including the policeman. Then my parents extracted a promise from me never to wander off like that again. But I did.

✦

"Memory believes before knowing remembers. Believes longer than recollects, longer than knowing even wonders." That's Faulkner telling us that memory is an act of faith. I remembering you, you remembering me—these are acts of love driven by the imagination. We may not remember each other accurately. We may not remember each other at all. Yet we remember loving.

✦

Who have you truly loved? Truly. Not the ones you holler "Love you!" to as you depart a restaurant or a home in which you've eaten an especially satisfying dinner of lamb chops. Not the ones to whom you sign "Love you" on a thank-you note or the old friends to whom you write "Love you" at the ends of letters— those friends who might expect nothing less than your love after all these long years.

Not these but rather the few, the very few, for whom your love runs so deep it is a silence, a stream behind a house in Vermont. The few who congregate around your heart and stand together in a circle, like the deacons of a church—though in reality these few may not know one another. All they have in common is you and your true love. They are you. They know one another tacitly as you.

And because they are your true loves, you are theirs. They know you—what is the phrase?—better than you know yourself. If you need to know yourself better than you already do, you go to them. They guess your every move, your next misstep. They advise and consent or disagree and steer you right. They never let you down.

I think of them, the few I truly love, on this winter night, under the tangled stars and the clouds' shadows—this night with the voices of the surf choir singing to a vast bruise of the sea. And when the moon is cold.

✦

Why should I care that the cook who feeds the gaunt and ghost-eyed men and women at the Upper West Side homeless shelter where I volunteer prepares everything with scoops of lard, including the eggs, including the orange juice? Why should I care? He's only killing the already as-good-as-dead. The surplus population.

But that's just it, you see. If there's no effort, even the most apparently casual gesture to suggest to these folks that they too deserve to be saved from a lethal diet, why should they think that they have a right to remark on wheeling owls in Riverside Park, or to dream into the mottled waters of the Hudson, or to try to make sense of the swarm of show-tune lyrics that attacks them like wasps in the middle of the night.

We are responsible for each other, even if the cook tells me to mind my own business.

✦

In Sudan in 1992, writing about the "Lost Boys" for *Vanity Fair*, I came upon a clearing a few hours after a large group of boys had arrived there. They were escaping the soldiers of the Khartoum government that had murdered their parents and enslaved their sisters. On their flight south, they had encountered dangerous animals, rains, swollen rivers, starvation, and disease. I held an eleven-year-old in my arms who was dying of a fever and a lack of food. He weighed nothing.

When I entered the campgrounds, the boys had already started to settle in, pitching tents and scouring the area for anything to eat. I told them who I was and what I was doing there. As I chatted with a few of them, several others went to work building me a bed and a table and setting up a *tukul*, a small hut, for me to stay in. To do so, they had to pause in their efforts to provide for themselves.

All of this was done without ceremony or anything that drew attention to their considerate generosity. No matter how dire their circumstances, I was their guest, someone to look after and make comfortable before they did anything for themselves. They were responsible for my well-being. Such gentle people.

✦

Like a baby stillborn, like a beast with his horn,
I have torn everyone who reached out for me.
—LEONARD COHEN

Me too. I must stop.

Love calls us to the things of this world.
—RICHARD WILBUR

That's better.

✦

This will floor you. At the railway station in Kanpur, India, a monkey fell on an electrical wire and was electrocuted. Seeing the accident, another monkey, presumably a friend, picked up the victim off the wire and tried resuscitating him by shaking him, punching him, and dipping his frizzled, blackened body in the water. The other monkeys sat around on various perches in the railway station, spectators, watching what seemed certain was a futile effort at rescue. The fallen monkey was dead. That was that.

Then, after a very long effort, the electrocuted monkey sat up straight, alive. Clearly shaken but alive. His friend kept touching him, nudging him, perhaps to assure them both that the he was indeed OK. That's all there is to the story, which nonetheless traversed all of India. Commentators attached the event to a myth involving ancient Indian gods. But it was simply a tale of one creature never giving up on another. Bang the drum slowly, until the heart beats again, in perfect monkey rhythm.

✦

Jazzmen like Bill Evans and Miles Davis (as if there could be anyone like them) are masters of the ostinato, the repeated phrase or theme. So practiced are they in this art that five levels of ostinatos can be reached and detected at once. The effect is a mystery. You remember hearing something that you hear for the first time. One may try for that effect in writing, too. Life, love, and responsibility. In the ostinatos of these fragments, can you make out the tune?

✦

On the other side of the table in the restaurant, Seng and Sreymom work on their salads and look at me like expectant children. The couple are in their early thirties. Twenty-two years have passed since I first met Seng at the Khao-I-Dang Refugee Camp in Thailand, to which he had escaped as a boy from Pol Pot's slaughterhouse. As a man he looks much as he did then—more aware and a little weary yet still sweet and respectful. His ears protrude like the handles of brown coffee cups. His eyes are dark and searching, like a scholar's. So are his wife's. The two met and married in Massachusetts, both of them part of a community of Cambodians who lived in the area around Lowell. Sreymom goes to nursing school. Seng is a guidance counselor, helping other Cambodian refugees. They remark that they are enjoying their salads.

It is so strange, wonderfully strange, to be sitting across from Seng in this serene, sun-quiet Manhattan bistro. We came into each other's lives when I was writing a cover story called "Children of War" for *Time* magazine in 1982 that later became a book of the same title. Now Seng has written a book of his own about his life in Cambodia. The occasion of our lunch is to celebrate its completion. I realize I am observing a miracle, in a French restaurant in New York in America—a time travel removed from the world of the little boy in Khao-I-Dang.

Children of War dealt with a great many children surviving in half a dozen war zones, but the publisher chose the photograph of Seng for the cover. The reason, I believe, is that even at his young age, Seng's face showed a determination to survive, combined with a concern for others, a useful gentleness amid horror. Seng's father had been killed by a firing squad because he was a doctor, thus an intellectual, thus an enemy of the state the Khmer Rouge had made mad. A few years later, his mother had died of starvation. At the age of eight, Seng oversaw her burial in their village. He wrote in his diary, "Dear Friend, I turn to you in my hour of sorrow and trouble."

Seng was rescued from the refugee camp because "Children of War" happened to be read by a Massachusetts family who became his foster parents. Seng was lucky, and so was I; happy consequences of journalism are rare. Only a few years ago did I first see him again, grown purposeful and confident in his adulthood and loving marriage. And yet, as he stood in my doorway after all those years, it was clear that the child was the father of the man. I would have known him anywhere.

At our lunch, I tell Seng that I have framed the drawing he made for me at Khao-I-Dang. It hangs near my writing desk. In the camp I asked him if he would do a self-portrait, but instead he produced a drawing of a bright blue airplane with a green door, green engine and nose and tail. I asked him where he was in the drawing. "I am the pilot!" he said. "We are flying to France!" His eyes were wide with hope and expectation, as they are now, in the bistro. He wonders how his book will be received. I think I can tell him. It will be received for what it is—a tale of life born of death.

✦

"We live in one another's shadow"—an Irish saying that, like all things Irish, cuts several ways at once. We live in one another's shadow, meaning we follow on one another, as in the act of shadowing. Or "shadow" as in shade, creating a canopy of protection of one person by another. Or as in foreshadowing, suggesting that the course of one life predicts the course of another. The shadow knows. Or as in diminished stature, when one person appears unable to get out from under the shadow of another. Or as in accepting something flimsy or shallow, shadow rather than substance.

But I see the idea of the shadow as wholly expansive and giving. Something projected from us, at once our image and companion, that constantly and lovingly makes connections to our fellows. We live in one another's shadow—the shadow being something that extends one's being. The way a shadow, cast upon the ground, precedes us when the sun is behind us or accompanies us along a city wall. We live in the extension and projection of one another, each person constructed to reach toward someone else. We touch, my shadow and I. And yours.

✦

"Speech! Speech!"

In the tidal wave to come and in the earthquake, typhoon; in the Cambodian abattoir; in the Black Plague and the snow squall and the forest fire and the flood; and in the incessant shouting and blasting of dynamite, I would like to detect some serene center, a cool, serene center, like the cork in a baseball, along with the frail hope that when the dust of the destroyers settles into a fine old layer cake, the center will attract the poets and pitchers, who will make of it something useful. A mass revolution. Wouldn't that be something? Wouldn't that be the *best*? Then we will no longer pick at history's scabs. Then we will rid ourselves of the debauchery of consciousness, free ourselves of the burden of self. And no more will the world be as one observes it to be—murderous, unforgiving, and sad. It will be more like a cosmos of roses, blooming on the parapets, or in the vestries of the Shropshire churches, or in the victory gardens on Delancey Street. Reconcile beauty with horror? Don't make me laugh. But the hour of true reconciliation will arrive. I am certain of it. This will happen. This will be a happening. My dreams stand sentry-like in a lichened grove while I salute the newborn child, the newborn us. Playful noises? Rational argument? Meaningful work? A mastery over menaces? By then, I will have long put away my pens and ink, and I shall go for walks on the beach and greet small nervous birds when I am not otherwise occupied cleaning sea bass or playing pepper or pickle with my grandchildren. And when I peer into the path of the Cold Moon, the silver cities will shine back at me while Schumann plays something somewhere. So I shall invent a new syntax and be pleased with my thoughts. O my love. O my stranger. From here on in, I rag nobody.

(*Applause. A smattering.*)

✦

I am six. Rutherford Platt, a renowned naturalist, is taking his sons Ruddy and Andy along with me and a group of the neighborhood boys for a nature tour of Central Park. His sons are proud of him. It impresses me that a famous man who knows so much is willing to share his time and knowledge with other people's children. We walk hurriedly from sight to sight in the park. Mr. Platt looks like a bald cleric, with a welcoming smile and a scrutinizing gaze. He points out various types of trees and rocks. I do not think we boys are expected to learn all this. I think he means us to appreciate what nature gives to the city. We try to absorb his enthusiasm. He tells us about Frederick Law Olmsted and extols the foresight of the landscape architect who created a sanctuary for the natural world in the center of the steel towers before there were steel towers.

The group swings one way and then the other, like sheep herded by a dog. I am lagging in the back. Then Mr. Platt and the other boys are gone. Just like that. And I am standing on a path alone as bicy-clists wheel by. I make no effort to catch up with the group. Instead, I wander, taking note of everything around me, especially the people. Families with baby carriages. Solitary walkers and lovers. A park custodian with a garbage pail on rollers greets me cheerily and moves on. Finally (after an hour? ten minutes?) a tall policeman spots me, takes me to the park station house, and gives me an orangeade. He speaks into a microphone on a desk. Over the PA system, he announces, "We have an unaccom-panied minor." He calls out my name and describes my clothing.

Soon Mr. Platt and the others show up at the station. I am glad to see them, though as I took in the life of the park, I never was fearful. "We lost you," says Mr. Platt, looking something between terrified and studious. "Or, did you lose *us*?"

✦

Night falls; night rises. The saffron moon settles into its slot as if the sky were a pinball machine. You even see it wobble before coming to rest. I watch the waves grab at the individual figments of light and then present them to the others like a trophy cup. My candle drips wax on the celestial staircase. All yearnings are subdued. All gripes. What joy to be a

husband, a father, a grandfather, a friend, a writer,
a teacher, alive.

✦

VESPERS

Blessed be the Cold Moon.
Blessed be the boulevard of light.
Blessed be the tides.
Blessed be the natural world.
Blessed be the natural world and its hidden
    secrets—the unripe seed, the pregnant
    animal, the inspiration in its incubator, the
    Lost Boys of Sudan, all life out of sight.
Blessed be the missing persons.
Blessed be invisibility.
Blessed be breath.
Blessed be your longing.
Your longing and your wanderings.
Blessed be Seng.
Blessed be your longing without belonging.
    Your endless searching.
Blessed be your eyes in their endless searching.
And your surprise.
And your lies. Blessed be them, too.
And your kindness and your gentleness.
And your bandages.

Blessed be the bandages you affix to the
    wounds of others.
Blessed be the wounds.
Blessed be the others.

✦

Boots baking dry in the mudroom; life; ice slivers glit-
tering at the side of a canal; sap drizzles from a dying
star; Concerto in F coming from a practice cottage
in Chautauqua, played by Gershwin himself, no less;
and I am not a soldier anymore; I am a farmer; I am
a microchimeric cell; a cloudburst surprises a pig, his
snout reacting upward; bright coal; a cuppa tea; the
leg and the egg; a word from Philo; life; just lay the
comb and brush on the dressing table; your dog's all
right; you're all right; an oak beam splayed beneath
a cracked shutter; sprouts; wax; did you remember
the milk?; did you remember the honey?; life; walk
with me to the shore?; red, right, returning; beat the
wheat into flames; cloud streaks over San Antonio;
life; a madman hurtles toward the swimming pond,
bearing a torch once used in the 1936 Olympics; hide
the children; a wedding ring discovered in a gutter;
frets discovered on Mars; life; if language fails, fall
back to the music in the looms; that is, if language
fails; our daughter Amy dies at age thirty-eight; love
calls us to the things of this world.

My aunt Julia was small and bent from osteoporosis, and she walked with much difficulty, though you couldn't tell, because her bright "Hello" ran interference for her. She worked at her secretarial job her whole life, taking two weeks' vacation in the summers in Kennebunkport, Maine. The proprietor of the hotel she stayed in gave Julia her room for free, simply because he liked her. Who could not like my aunt Julia? She was life itself, in a small package. An amateur painter, she brought her canvases to Kennebunkport, and her easel and oils, and she spent the long bright days painting the sea. She wore big jewelry and turbans.

One summer when I was fifteen, out of the blue, Julia asked if I would like to join her in Kennebunkport. Without hesitation I said yes. Those were the summers I worked at a tedious job for my grandfather, watching over a dead office and playing pickup basketball in nearby playgrounds. Two weeks with Julia seemed just the ticket.

We took the train to Kennebunkport. The hotel proprietor, a burly man whose face was barely visible under a cloud of gray whiskers, greeted Julia with a bear hug that hoisted her high in the air. She smiled demurely. "We love to have your aunt here," the proprietor told me. "This hotel has been around one hundred sixty-two years. Four US presidents have stayed with us. Winston Churchill, too. Even the queen of Denmark. But Julia Spruch is our favorite guest. She is *real* aristocracy."

My room had a small terrace with a direct view of the ocean. It occurred to me that it must have cost a good deal, but poor as Julia was, she never mentioned money, certainly not the lack of it. We had all our meals together. She told me about spending her days painting. I told her about my solitary walks and about meeting some kids from Boston on a beach. One girl had asked me if I was a MOT, "a member of our tribe," meaning Jewish. I had never heard the acronym. Julia asked what I'd said to the girl. "I told her I'm not the member of any tribe," I said.

Julia patted my hand. "That's right," she said.

"I'm painting something for you," she told me.

"A portrait?" I asked. She specialized in portraits—often of strangers, people she happened to meet. Everyone interested her, attracting her sympathies. She loved people naturally, and she saw their worth. "I'm sure I'll love it," I said. On the morning of our departure, she led me to the side porch where she had been working those two weeks. A hotel bath towel was draped over the canvas so that Julia could unveil her artistry with mock ceremony.

Many years later, when she was dying, I used to hear her screams of pain in the hospital hall before I got to her room. The screams would stop abruptly when I entered and she saw me. Then she would smile and offer me the meal on the tray she had not touched. In a faint voice, she would ask how I was doing, what I was doing. Whatever I told her, no matter how insignificant, was greeted with joyful surprise. She never went silent. As I was leaving one afternoon, she asked if I ever looked at the portrait of me she had done in Kennebunkport—me standing on a terrace looking out at the sea and one lone sailboat. "Only every day," I told her.

At a small memorial service in the office in which she had worked, her colleagues spoke of her warmly. Each said something different, emphasizing a particular quality of my aunt's, but there was no question that they were speaking of the same person. Her boss went last. He said, "Julia was very small, and she lived in a very small compass, but the world of her heart was immeasurable, because she filled every inch with life, love, and care for others." My aunt Julia.

✦

Christa Reinig wrote that she had a whiskey bottle and a coffeepot and a chessboard with the pieces poised to be moved but no one to move them and no one to visit her. Ever read Christa's poems? She wrote that she had an endless sky above her where she might find herself again, and a city full of streets where she might meet herself, and an endless song to sing. But in fact, she had no more than the smallest plot of land, with a single sunflower growing out of the lightning crack in the sidewalk, and she had to live there.

✦

From the age of thirteen through the end of high school, I delve into the old bookshops on lower Fourth Avenue, my eyes adjusting as I enter the caves. Not black exactly, the shelves sagging with books. Not green exactly, the bindings. Not brown either, not exactly, but rather a dappled gray that becomes as much one color as the other, depending on what little light seeps inside. The bald heads of the old socialist proprietors are buried in their newspapers. Their green eyeshades conceal their faces. They do not acknowledge me, yet they recognize me—another kid smitten with the smell and taste of books. Most days I browse. Some days I buy. One dollar, maybe two—for a biography of Napoleon or a collection of Shakespeare's history plays shrunken in a leather-bound volume the size of one's fist. Most days I poke around like a botanist in the rain forest.

Dark, dark. Today I buy Rilke's *Letters to a Young Poet*, though I do not know Rilke's work and only guess that he's a poet by the fact that he has written these letters. It is pouring, and I have neither hat nor umbrella. Unsuccessfully, I try to protect my brown wrapping paper from the slanting rain. In my room, I place the sodden book on newspaper and wait days before the pages dry out and can be separated. One morning, a sentence rises, as if during a séance, insisting that I read it: "Therefore, dear Sir, love your solitude, and try to sing out with the pain it causes you."

✦

My three-windowed wall takes in the broad face and sullen gaiety of the sea. Windows are portals, ports. In Beirut in 1982, after a car bomb had skinned the facade of buildings on an entire block, killing sixty or seventy and choking the air with gray sulfurous smoke, I looked away and saw a boy, age ten or so, sitting at a window, taking in the scene. No expression on his face. No shock or fear. Just looking. Children at windows everywhere, watching and unconsciously learning how the world is. We are children at windows.

In my dreadful school, I sat at a desk at the end of a row of desks, where I could look out a very large window and see a thousand shades of green in the trees. That window became my school. The eyes, they say, are windows to the soul. Yet windows work two ways. What does the soul see looking outward? What do I see out the three windows of my wall when I take in the broad face and sullen gaiety of the sea.

✦

Ingenuity is impressive, irrespective of its uses. Don't you think? I mean, how those divers in Thailand figured out a way to extricate the boys' soccer team trapped in a cave, moving over two miles underwater through snakelike caverns. Swaddling the boys to protect them in the water. Ingenious.

But no more so than the English in colonial America who gave smallpox-infected blankets to the Native Americans, to exterminate the race. Or the person who invented the cluster bomb. I saw how it worked in Beirut. A child grows curious about a metal object lying on the ground. He touches it and the cluster bomb rises straight up, three feet in the air, just the height of a child. Then, because the bomb is composed of a compact cluster of metal fragments, it explodes like a hailstorm. Bye-bye, baby. Impressive. No?

Think of how much ingenuity went into the

creation of the A Bomb. Starting from the work of Einstein, Oppenheimer, and Fermi, many of the best scientific minds in the country clustered at Los Alamos and figured out how free neutrons hitting the nucleus of a uranium atom would result in the most destructive weapon ever made. In the Hiroshima Peace Memorial Museum, one may inspect the consequences of the work. Pictures of melting flesh. Horses with their legs blown off. A molten pocket watch.

Breathtaking, all the uses people make of their creative thinking. Rachmaninoff, Gershwin, the divers in Thailand, Bach, Vermeer, the inventor of the cluster bomb, Oppenheimer, Einstein, Wordsworth, Shakespeare. Knocks your socks off. Would they be impressed with one another, say, at a convention of ingenious geniuses? Would they sit around one of the lethally boring tables at Aspen and applaud one another for their insights, for the way each of them surveyed a situation and proceeded to change it dramatically. Would Vermeer slap Fermi on the back and say, "Way to go, man!" In Dutch, of course.

And yet I look at you, and all these people disappear. Yesterday, for instance, when we were having breakfast in the diner, and you looked at our fiftysomething Latina waitress, with her morning smile competing with her exhausted eyes, and then at me. "Do we have a hundred dollars to leave her for a tip?" you said. And when our waitress could not believe what we did and kept looking alternately at the money and at us and you said, "A New Year's gift" to remove the sting of charity from the gesture. You did all that with your ingenious eye and your ingenious heart. Impressive.

✦

Termites are impressive. In the building of a termite hill, when all the uprights are in place, the termites instinctively know that it's time to turn the arch. All the termites take to the task at just about the same time. Architecturally, it is exactly the right time to do it in order to get the necessary ventilation and air conditioning in the hill. Timing. If you do not act at the moment the opportunity presents itself, you are one dead termite. But termites are responsible for each other.

✦

I am four. It is August 15, 1945, and the war has just ended. Japan has surrendered. We are on the beach at the Cape, and my parents and I huddle around the portable radio to listen to the celebrations in Times Square. I know little about the war, except for what I've heard in radio broadcasts of body counts. There are signs in grocery stores: "No eggs, no arguments." Lines at the pump. I like listening to the Andrews Sisters singing "Boogie Woogie Bugle Boy" and looking at pictures of women in their sassy red Rosie the Riveter bandanas. In the city, we have the occasional air-raid drill. My father is an air-raid warden. As a doctor, he examines recruits. He's tried to enlist, but color blindness keeps him out of the service. I think the army gives him the rank of captain anyway. Now the three of us listen to the shouting and the horns. My parents are happy, so I am happy.

Forty years later I am on Tinian, the island from which the *Enola Gay* took off. The island is half airstrip—the length necessary for the bomber to gain altitude while carrying the excessive weight of the bomb. Weeds grow in the fissures of the runway. Another fretted terrain. The air is dank. The previous night, I patrolled the beach in Saipan, picking up spent shells, unclaimed souvenirs of battles. I seem always to be collecting shells. The cover essay I will write for *Time* will be called "My God, What Have We Done?"—reported to be the words of Captain Robert Lewis, the copilot of the *Enola Gay*. I will write of him, and of a man named Kawamoto in Hiroshima who, as a boy, survived the bombing, and of a physicist named Agnew who flew in the instruments plane beside the *Enola Gay* on the morning of August 6, 1945. As I begin to write, I will realize what "Enola" spells backward.

On August 15, 1945, I have my first feelings about belonging to big events. Things happening thousands of miles away affect Cape Cod. The air is an ocean breeze. I dig for clams and observe my parents in the world's temporary peace.

✦

The selkies. You've heard of them? The female sea spirits who lived on earth like ordinary people but whose true home was the sea? Much more interesting and complicated than mermaids, selkies could maintain contact with humans only for a certain amount of time. While on earth they made excellent wives and mothers, but since they belonged to the sea, they eventually would grow sullen and depressed and would return to their world under water. People who had not recognized that they were selkies all along thought the women were drowning by accident. What the onlookers were observing, in fact, was simply a homecoming. The selkies saw their lives on earth as indentured servitude. To survive as themselves, they had to go home.

✦

"It was so whimsical," she said, recalling a moment many years ago when she and Amy decided, on the spur of the moment, to take a horse and buggy ride through Central Park. Then she—the most beautiful, the most thoughtful, the most tender—wept in silence, longing for the whimsical.

✦

One thing you can say about the sea: it resists resolution. In turmoil, in a murmur, under a typhoon, in the doldrums, it moves constantly, without any indication that it seeks a single shape, goal, or purpose. It does not wish to take a position. To the contrary, it clearly, actively wishes to take no position, or to take every position at once, which makes the sea like poetry. Like art in general. Art gives shape to irresolution. Everything resolved by nothing resolved.

Something implied in this, I think: the act of resisting resolution suggests limits to knowing. The motions of the waves, the motions of the mind, keep life at sea. No answers here. No answers in a poem by, say, Wallace Stevens. There is this possibility; there is that. Both coexist in a comfortable discomfort.

What do I mean when I speak of the world? What size object do I have in mind? Something so huge, one cannot wrap one's arms around it? Or wrap a thought around it? Something so small, one can hold it in the palm of one's hand, like a single tear. That's what happened in *Stairway to Heaven*. A man's soul was rescued from death by a handheld tear. "I am a little world made cunningly," John Donne announced. All in one. I am limited without limits.

How strangely calming it is to watch the sea, cresting, unquesting, content in its eternally restless self. To seek without any ambition to find—love is a bit like that. We live in one another's shadow.

✦

Beauty stays in my head, fresh as a daisy, bright as a brand-new penny. A tenant with squatter's rights, it never leaves. Why is that? Bad temper does not stay in my head. Good health does not stay in my head. In a time of illness, I cannot recall what it felt like to be robust, in the pink. Similarly, I cannot recall pain. No one can. You remember that something hurt, yet you can feel it no longer.

But beauty—I mean like the cowled elm disguised as a monk on the front lawn, or the wings of the magnolia, or a handkerchief of grass beside the swimming hole, or peat, or pitch. Such things hold their positions, like dancers told to "Freeze." Frieze. Take tonight on the sea. A permanent frieze of whitecaps. An establishment of terns.

Sometimes I just miss everyone. Those I hated, those I barely knew. Along with loved ones. Each one takes the name of a flower. And they are with me too, standing among all the other beautiful things in the inventory. Songs as well. "September Song." "Where or When," Even where or when I am weary, they remain. Even then.

It takes over eight minutes for light to travel from Earth to the sun. It starts with me. Cool stars. Cold Moon. A projection of the face of Eva Marie Saint as she discloses the secret beauty of Marlon Brando in *On the Waterfront*. A projection of Harpo Marx's adoring eyes on the harp strings in *A Day at the Races*. He plays "Blue Venetian Waters."

✦

Nothing is gone. Nothing. Not the tide. Not the moon. Not your Amy, or your aunt Julia, or your sixth birthday party where you stood on your chair and sang "Blue Skies." Not your sins, either. Some things you want gone forever. Some you want to retrieve and keep in your purse or your safe-deposit box. Whatever you want or do not want makes no difference. No difference. Nothing is gone.

And Philip Larkin's line "What will survive of us is love"? That is not gone, either. Not the line. Not the thought. What will survive of us is love.

＋

Stet, your outstretched hand. Fix, my frosty silence. Stet, your quiet fire. Fix, my conflagration. Fix, my boiling point. Stet, your understanding, your patience in the storm's eye. Stet, your courage. Fix, my weakness and my fright. Fix, my hair-trigger wit, too fast, too sharp. Fix, my jumping-bean mind. Fix, my speech to the jury. Stet, the verdict of your sympathy. Stet, your tender kiss. Fix, my slamming of the door. Fix, my noisy ghosts. Stet, your orchids, your porcelain vase, your sweet-smelling cheeks. Fix, your tears. Fix, "I love you." Stet, "I love you."

＋

Pardon my appearance. I'm old. I may miss a whisker or two when shaving. And I can't do a thing with what's left of my hair. My socks don't always match. My fly was at half-mast one day last week, when I emerged from the men's room in an Italian restaurant, the one I like on Second Avenue, or is it Third? My short-term memory is not what it used to be. I'm growing shorter myself, if one can grow shorter. And when I studied the bathroom mirror this morning, the lines on my face looked like fissures in the Gobi desert. Cracks in the driest terrain. That's me. Not too shabby, but shabby.

I don't know what to make if it. Old age, I mean. I'm no Rabbi Ben Ezra. The best is yet to be? Depends what you mean by best. Not the best use of similes or metaphors anymore. That's for sure. Not the best verbs. A few good nouns from time to time. But nothing to write home about. Nothing to write anywhere about. The appreciation of other writers. That seems to be improving. The appreciation of others generally. I never was big on envy. But even the faint wistful wuffles of jealousy have gone. Presto. Like a magician's rabbit. See what I mean about similes and metaphors? "Like a magician's rabbit." And "wistful wuffles"? Jesus.

Pardon my appearance? It is what it is, as they say. What you see is what you get, as they say. I wear no other face. No young man's unattractive ambition or noisy despair. No dying man's Jacob Marley–like recriminations or pathetic lusts or vengeful sarcasms and complaints. Old age is the only purely realistic stage of life. The stage when one is glad to inhabit the Gobi desert and quietly celebrate the cracks. Every crack a Gobi rushing river in the driest terrain. The cool example of old age. Who would condescend to pardon such stunning, breathtaking beauty?

✦

At first light, I will go to the piano and play "September Song." It's on my play-by-ear list. I have always played jazz piano by ear, never having bothered to learn to read music. I know I should have. If I could read music, my ear playing would be so improved, as I would hear what the song originally intended one to hear, and riff from there. Yet there are advantages to playing the way I do. I never play a tune the same way twice. Every tune is an invitation to improvisation, like jazz itself. Jazz is the art of improvisation. When I make a mistake, I deliberately follow it with another mistake, to make the first one seem intentional. One can do that with life. The days grow cold when you reach September.

Walter Huston sang "September Song" on Broadway, in *Knickerbocker Holiday* (1938). Kurt Weill and Maxwell Anderson wrote the music and the book respectively, based loosely on Washington Irving's *Father Knickerbocker Stories* about life in New Netherland in the seventeenth century. Huston played Peter Stuyvesant, governor of New Amsterdam, who is in love with a much younger woman, Tina Tienhoven. At first the governor tries to pressure Tina into marrying him. Eventually he gives her up to a younger man. Of course, "September Song" has a wider application than to one particular love story.

We approach Perihelion Day, January 5, when

the Earth makes its closest approach to the sun. On January 10 comes the Wolf Moon Eclipse, the penumbral lunar eclipse of the first full moon of the year. The Cold Moon augurs the Wolf Moon.

✦

Ralph Ellison's *Invisible Man* spoke of living on the nodes of the blues, the way Louis Armstrong played. Ellison knew writing and jazz. Music lives between the notes. Writing, between the words. And love in the space you leave me.

✦

This kid—I still can see his face, like petrified wood. I am twelve or thirteen. I am riding my bike in Central Park. I am not riding on the path designated for bikes. Neither is this kid. I am in corduroys and a bright blue sweater and brand-new Keds. This kid is in work pants, work shoes, and a dirty T-shirt. He is pale, wiry, and needs a haircut. A cop standing where we ride by calls out, "Hey!" This kid and I both stop. The cop ignores me, but he goes straight to this kid and slaps him hard in the face with his flat palm. You can hear the echo. Then he unscrews the valves on this kid's tires and gives the bike two flats. "Ride on the bike path," he says to this kid, whose face is maroon from the slap.

The cop walks away without looking at me. But I look at the kid. He does not cry or whine or say a word, until he sees me staring. "What are you looking at?" he says.

✦

EVA MARIE SAINT. Shouldn't everybody care about everybody else?
MARLON BRANDO. What a fruitcake you are!
EVA MARIE SAINT. I mean, isn't everybody a part of everybody else?
—from *On the Waterfront*

✦

Manny's Optical. A no-more-than-fifteen-foot-wide hole-in-the-wall in midtown on First Avenue. How did it get there? Well, it started with Manny, of course, and his ambition to study to be an optician and open a place of his own. What to call it? Manny's Optical. A clean, straightforward name, like Manny himself, a stand-up guy. Position yourself before Manny's, with the tiers of eyeglasses in the little display window, and there is no doubt where you are. You need a good pair of glasses? You need Manny's Optical.

You need Manny. That's the other thing. You need someone who wanted to create a useful life. To have his own spot on earth, like Christa Reinig but without Christa's wider vision. Yet Manny had vision, his own vision and, in his mind, yours and mine. Manny had a modest, generous thought—to help everyone see clearly, just as Manny saw. His life, his limits, his limitlessness.

Manny's Optical is the cosmos to Manny, and to Mrs. Manny, and to Manny's little boy and girl, Danny and Fanny. And you are part of Manny's universe. Manny's could not exist without you and your poor eyes. Bless your eyes. So you coexist, you and Manny, even if you may never enter his shop. And you may not. It is, after all, only a hole-in-the-wall on First Avenue. And yet, how well one sees, how clear as blue daylight one sees, after a visit to Manny's Optical.

✦

Rivers in the sky. Did I read that correctly? Rivers in the atmosphere that dwarf the Amazon and the Nile, carrying moisture from Portugal to South Africa to Chile to us, causing storms, snows, floods. In February 2019, an atmospheric river propelled an avenue of water vapor 350 miles wide and 1,600 miles long. In dry conditions, these rivers can replenish water supplies. In wet conditions, they can kill you.

Hope is like that. In impossible situations, hope

can suck out your heart. We hope against hope. In better times, we ride on the river in the sky and sing. Hope springs eternal. Hope is the thing with feathers. The bird that sees the glass door in the kitchen for what it is, acknowledges that the door is made of glass, yet flies through, unharmed, exultant.

Life hopes. Love hopes. We are responsible for each other's hope.

✦

What did you do?
    Me?
    What did you do?
    You must have me mistaken for someone else.
    What did you do?
    Nothing! I did nothing!
    Exactly.

✦

The life you never led had a trip to Venice in it and a fifty-third-place finish in the Boston Marathon and a girl named Faye and a deep-sea exploration that brought you face-to-face with the *Vampyroteuthis infernalis* and its hypnotic blue eyes. Instead, you had to settle for a life that included a trip to Venice, a fifty-third-place finish in the Boston Marathon, a girl named Faye, and a deep-sea exploration that brought you face-to-face with the *Vampyroteuthis infernalis* and its hypnotic blue eyes.

+

Mars on the horizon. I cannot make out the fretted terrain. To my poor eyesight, the planet appears a halo of Christmas lights, like a bejeweled tiara with a prominent ruby atop the rim. Along the celestial arc beams Venus, too, another bright light but without the red. In *Between Mars and Venus*, poet Robert Conquest wrote of the "kindred themes" imposed by the two planets on the human imagination. The twin worlds of knowledge and art were evoked by Drake and Shakespeare, the two Wills. Conquest said "cultures turn rotten" when those themes grow apart from each other. The conjoining of scientific and artistic exploration, on the other hand, "gives us the endless sky."

Say you are knowledge. Say I am art. Say the sky's the limit.

+

Is the Internet a classic shrink? Positioning a Dictaphone on the coffee table, staring quasi-passively, quasi-sympathetically, as you drone on. Good morning, Dr. Internet.

Everything you do is recorded somewhere. It

lives, somewhere. You don't remember half the things you said—the truths, the lies, the half lies (they're the worst)—but scroll down far enough, and voilà, there they are, good as new, bright as a penny. Your loud pronouncements. Your demurrers. Your PSs, bar mitzvah speeches, boasts, wisecracks, oaths, abject apologies, everything verbal and pictorial. There. Available eventually as you scan your own inventory.

Does Judgment Day follow? Not at all. Good morning, Dr. Internet. Everything just sits there, every word, every confession, like wet stones in a creek, without anyone shouting, "That was right!" "That was bad!" "That was you, poor slob. Can you believe it! *You* said that. You were *there*, saying *that*."

Yesterday, as if lurching out of a dark alley, there I was on my iPad, giving a public reading from *Kayak Morning*, the book I wrote about Amy two and a half years after she died. The money people at my publishing house hadn't wanted any part of it. Referring to *Making Toast*, my book about our family after Amy's death, the money people had said, "We've already heard him on the subject of grief." My editor prevailed.

The reading, the lectern, brought it all back in a rush—what I had written, what had happened, me in my kayak, in the creek, up the creek, with a paddle.

Everything you do is recorded somewhere by Dr. Internet. For better or worse, you are in a constant state of rebirth. In *Kayak Morning*, I wrote that water is the earth's only self-renewing resource. Wrong again.

✦

Wet cement in a square of sidewalk at the southeast corner of the park. I am ten. I take the eraser end of a pencil and carve my initials, hoping one of the sidewalk repair workers doesn't see me. I write the *R*s in block letters, making them noticeable. I will walk by here in twenty or thirty years and see proof of my life, of my existence.

✦

The Kemp's ridley sea turtle, the smallest of the sea turtles, lays its eggs on the Gulf Coast of Mexico, in the state of Tamaulipas. Ravenous birds devour most of the eggs. The surviving turtles swim north all the way to the southern shores of Long Island, where they encounter spider crabs in a sort of pre-season scrimmage that allows them to gain strength for the main event. Many turtles perish in these encounters. But the ones that prevail are made strong enough to endure the next pilgrimage, to Chesapeake Bay in Maryland, where they do battle with full-size crabs. By this point, of course, there are many fewer turtles than when they started out from Mexico. It hardly comes as a surprise that the species is endangered, since their lives endanger them. The remaining sea turtles then make one final long swim back to Mexico, where they lay more eggs. And the cycle begins anew. All this activity is instinctive.

When I was working at *Time* magazine, there were many late nights spent going over copy and copyedited pieces. On such a night, I was in my office, waiting for my essay to come back from the copy editors. Around 1:00 a.m., I found myself looking directly across Fiftieth Street at an office containing another night owl, who was staring back at me. Two late-night workers in New York, taking each other in. At the very same time, each of us waved to the other. Nothing demonstrative or particularly friendly. Just the arm-extended, palm-up wave of silent mutual recognition in the dark of night.

In turtles and people, certain instincts are lifesavers.

✦

The heart is a warrior. Yes, it's true. I know you think the heart is soft, a pansy. But the heart is a warrior. Nothing to mess with. Hordes of hatreds and sorrows will attack you, teeth bared, and the faintest beat of the loving heart will drive them into submission. I know. I have seen it happen. I blister in a rage, and you love me in return. And all at once I am a Westie puppy on its back, and you are rubbing my tummy, and all I feel is the fierce power of your heart, my hero.

✦

When I was five, I developed an ear infection from swimming, and for a week I was not allowed to go in the water. My parents were vacationing in Westport, Connecticut, a small and sleepy town then. The local movie theater played one film a week, and the film running the week of my ear infection recovery was *Stairway to Heaven*. My mother took me to see it on Monday, and I found the film so beautiful and fascinating, I asked her to take me every day after that.

This was more an intuitive wish than a conscious decision. Instinctively, I felt the film was or would be valuable to me. Five hot summer afternoons in a row, in Westport, Connecticut, in 1946, watching *Stairway to Heaven*.

I don't know how much of the film I understood at that young age. I got the basic message about the restorative power of love. The moving staircase and the music made an especially powerful impression. Wide-eyed, I followed the marble steps ascending indefinitely as a piano played the highest and lowest notes in a quasi-ominous progression. I don't think I learned more with each successive day of the five I saw the movie. But there was something comforting in being with my mother regularly each afternoon and oddly exciting in knowing everything that was going to happen in the film before it did. The effect of anticipation over surprise.

The shifting back and forth from black and white to color as the story's locale changed from heaven to earth also pleased me. At the age of five, I had no doubt there was a heaven, so it seemed instructive to see what went on there. The historical person-ages who appeared. And the commanding figure of a woman who conducted the trial in which the battle for the soul was contested. And the bewigged judge, who quoted Sir Walter Scott's lines about love at the end of the film. It was all mysterious and thrilling to me. As was the sight of the single tear that became the crucial piece of evidence for the defense.

And being alone with my mother was half the fun. The following year, my brother would be born frail and sickly, and the attention of both my parents would be diverted to him—for all the remaining years of my childhood, really. But for that still, hot summer week in Westport, my mother belonged only to me. When, after the movie, we went to the soda parlor next to the theater, my mother would ask me if the movie had been as good that day as it had been the day before. "Better," I would say.

✦

In her essay, "The Death of the Moth," Virginia Woolf is in her study writing when she notices a moth in its death throes, batting about a small windowpane. The author watches the animal's struggle with pity and admiration—awe, really. The struggle is the inevitable one with death, the inevitable victor. Never lost a match. But Woolf focuses on life, the moth exerting all its tiny yet heroic powers to stave off what cannot be staved off. At one point, she attempts to right the moth with her pencil, but she can no more right the moth than write the moth. Tiny and insignificant as it is, the creature and its struggle are monumental, divine. In the end, Woolf imagines the moth telling death, you were too strong for me.

No subject is thought about or written about more than death and dying. There's something tantalizing about the certainty of death, far more assured than taxes. Yet the fascination with death, I think, has to do with what it gives to life. Death gives life to life. Woolf's moth was never so alive as it was in its final moments. My man Dick Wilbur said the strength of the genie comes from its being in a bottle. The containment forces a concentration on what is achieved by limitations. Thus, form in art. A cantata, a sonnet. A villanelle, such as "Do not go gentle into that good night." We gain life's powers by knowing they will be taken away.

✦

"Fearing to lose all," Joyce wrote in *A Portrait of the Artist as a Young Man.* Fearing to lose all, Stephen Dedalus reached for a pencil and paper. A life raft, such as might be used on the sea before me. A life raft, as he was drowning. With pencil and paper, he would write his villanelle. Does the act of writing cut the losses, hold them in check? Or does it make one aware of what is being lost, of the process of loss itself? It's a long, long time from May to December.

All poems are elegies at heart, at broken heart. Everything observed, everything that happens or has happened, about which you write, is attended by loss. As soon as your thought hits the paper, you lose it. As soon as your word hits the paper, you lose it. No wonder there is a feeling of perpetual dissatisfaction when one finishes a piece of writing. Fearing to lose all, you lose all anyway.

✦

A woman sits in the village square, which is a circle, in the circle she has made of herself, folding and stretching her body until she becomes the circle she sits in. She is the circle. Her eyes are brown. Her eyes are blue. She is your skin. Your next of kin. She is you, sitting where the wind has torn the light, like a pennant, heartbroken about the lover who has left her or pleased by the lover she has just met. Make of her what you will. She is an open book, the same old story, a tale told by an idiot; the play's the thing she is, a sonnet. She is impossible to read. Quiet as a novice, she looks upward for the whisper of wings. She is a miner in the coalpits, wearing her own light. She is a coachman bringing a gossipy dwarf to town. She is an owl in the rain, an intellectual's sigh, a plum, aplomb, a sweet, a rose, the Cold Moon. The heart's faint light exposes her as beautiful.

Let's have a parable. Shall we? In a distant kingdom, in an ancient time, a king announced that he would give his daughter in marriage to the man who produced what all the people agreed was the most incredible thing. (This is a Hans Christian Andersen story.) As the competition got underway, a modest young man stepped forward. He had created a wondrous clock, with each of the hours represented by figures from the Bible and other items of folklore and of common knowledge. At one o'clock, Moses was shown inscribing the first of the Ten Commandments. At two o'clock, there were Adam and Eve. At three, the three Wise Men. At four, the four seasons. At five, the five senses. And so forth. The modest young man presented his exquisite clock to the king, and the king was about to present the young man with his daughter. All the people in the court agreed that the clock was the most incredible thing.

But just then, another man appeared on the scene—a vulgar brute, with cold eyes and a smile like death. From his hand dangled a huge sledge-hammer. Without a moment's hesitation, the brute strode up to the clock, and with a single blow of his hammer, he smashed the intricate work of art to dust. Gone. The biblical figures gone, the seasons gone, the senses gone. The effect of this act on the king and the courtiers was dramatic and terrible. No one could believe his eyes. The king looked at the remains of the clock. Then, slowly and sadly, he took his daughter's hand and placed it in the hand of the brute. "Sir," he told him, "by your wanton destruction of something beautiful you truly have done the most incredible thing. The most incredible thing."

✦

I am looking through a window that's a door, never having seen such a thing before. I am five. It is the beginning of the summer of *Stairway to Heaven*, the day of our arrival in Westport. My parents are settling in when I decide to take one of my wandering walks. I come to the house with a window that's a door. Tall and wide, it is part of an entire window-wall, the wall of a solarium, though of course I have never seen one of those before, either.

What I have seen before is the Steinway. Only this one is a concert grand. It has the gleam of a black stallion, standing serenely powerful in the middle of the room. I open the door-window, enter the room that smells of roses, sit at the piano, and play my repertoire—"The Blue Danube" and "Londonderry Air." My legs dangle from the little chair that serves as a stool. I'm in a T-shirt and shorts.

She makes no sound when she enters, so the first moment I am aware of Ruth Steinkraus is when I glance up from the keys and see her smiling at the far end of the piano. I think she may be an illusion, so angelic does she look, wearing white and pale yellow and her hair blond like the sun. "Who are you?" she asks in a quiet, happy voice. "And where are your parents?" She gives me a dish of chocolate ice cream and then walks me back to the rented house. I'm not sure my parents knew I'd been gone.

"It's so unusual," she says to my mother. "Your son has no fear. He just walked into a strange house and played the piano."

My mother smiles quietly and nods. "It's the way he is," she says. "He thinks the world is waiting for him to walk in and play the piano."

✦

Moon sky. White waves. Will they ever come again? Bill Evans and Robert Conquest and Monk and Miles playing on *Kind of Blue*. Will they ever come again? Good people. Kind people. Books. Paints. Poems. Love songs. Will they ever come again? And you, hiding there behind the swales of the dunes. How about you? Bang the drum slowly. I hear the soft detonations of the stars.

✦

Puddles of fast fish; life; a Steinway concert grand; the branch of a mimosa in Houston; mist menacing the East River; slabs of red beef hanging on hooks in a walk-in freezer; an inspector calls; drains; life; the ruins of a manor house in Yonkers; cold herring in a Mason jar; say vespers in the moonlight; lulls of contrition; a stone in the shape of a brooding head reads the book of Exodus, in Hebrew; the mist of breath on a pane of glass; a street kid with a slapped face, maroon; where is the drowned girl?; where are the selkies?; petrified wood; petrified kittens; the destitution of stray lambs; the hypnotic blue eyes of the *Vampyroteuthis infernalis*; an ice sculpture of a pair of hands in prayer; a cloudburst surprises a sow, her snout reacting upward; life; walk with me to the shore; sing your heart out; sing "Don't Know Much"; in Scranton, crows hector a bull with a throbbing chest; he wishes he could fly; my mother's eggnog; a baker's dozen; an archive of shucked corn; life; and I am not a soldier anymore; I'm a beachcomber; Christa's sunflower grows out of a lightning crack in the sidewalk; a tumulus of old soda bottles; rain-soaked coal; sap seeps from a dying star; choke the wheat into flames; and a clatter of horses to the left and to the right, a roan in midjump over a beehive of rocks; life.

✦

Begin again, Mr. Carlyle? Is it possible? I dream I walk on the beach with a band of drunks, shouting and singing. They sing martial songs. I sing and drink with them. Goatherds pass. They wave. I wave. A chrysalis croons a ballad of transformation. I sing with it, as well. Cold Moon worshippers mumble in the gray light. I mumble with them. I seem to have the ability to adjust to any circumstance. In the middle distance, dogs bay at the pointed stars. I, too, bay. Horses plash at the lip of the shore, then gallop on the moraine of poetry. They are willful, ferocious. It is impossible to fling a rope around their necks and rein them in. I am changing as I watch them. I grow tusks, a beak, claws, fur, a snout. Do not bring me a mirror. I sprout hooves.

My papers? You demand to see my papers. They must be here somewhere. After all, I live among papers. Papers are my name. Papers are my game. So they must be here somewhere. When I find them, you will see that I am everything I purport to be.

You and me, for starters. I am you and me. And him over there, too. And her and it. That yellow lab. I am it. I am the dog and the kennel, to which I slink in the dark, like Dylan Thomas's hunchback in the park. And the Lost Boys of Sudan. And the beginning and the living end. The midsection, too. The solar plexus. The solar eclipse. The whole shebang, the livelong night and day (I am the one), and every sense, applied and not applied. And every cranny and every granny and every nook and every book. Every book. I mean it. I mean Melville. I mean Kerouac. I mean Elizabeth Hardwick and Djuna Barnes. And Emerson and Ellison and Wordsworth and Richard Wright. And Richard Wilbur. And Jimmy Baldwin.

Giving a reading with Baldwin once, I was very

young. He could tell I was nervous. He stage-whispered, "Don't worry, baby."

Every voice I am. Joni Mitchell's and Natalie Cole's. Along with the voices of those on the picket line, on the conga line, on the dotted line, and at the bus station, protesting the change of schedule. The bus driver is harassed by the mob. I am the mob. I am the driver. A child tumbles from the monkey bars. I am the monkey and the bars. The electrocuted monkey and the bars. I am the child. Where the train stops, I am the stop. Where the sand slides into the Atlantic under the Cold Moon, hanging over the static silver cities, I am that spot.

We will never again be what we were. I am that sentiment. We will be what we were, always. I am that sentiment, too. Those who live in the silver cities cannot hear the screams of the animals. I am that observation. What am I up to? You. What do I smell, taste, touch, ignore? You. But I also am you. And the white-washed post office. And the eland's entrails, stuck in the mouth of the lion. This and that. Hammacher Schlemmer. Sturm und Drang. And more. Infinitely more. I can prove it. Once I produce my papers, you will see that every claim of mine is true, valid, down to the nth degree, which I am, too. The nth degree.

✦

Are you OK? The standard question of the times. Are you OK? Am I? Sure, I'm OK. But are you? OK, I mean. Are you OK?

Know what's OK? Rain on the sea grass. That's OK. The damp sand and the iambic pace of the waves. Definitely OK. A starlit plow. A horse shies at the jump. A box of sweets. The spasms of parrots' heads. The survival of the Kemp's ridley turtle. Steam rising from cattle in the cold. A bolt of lightning. A bolt of fabric. The endless sky. All present but not always accounted for. No madmen here. No skulking tanks. Just you and your ledger, taking stock of the vowels and consonants of the earth. Somewhere else, men set steel traps for hares, splitting hares. But here everything is OK. Here, there is only the exonerating squeeze of the hand, wet sea grass, a glance of red berries, and your occasional weeping.

✦

Man! Can you believe it? This ocean, this Atlantic that scrolls out like an inky blueprint of the universe, is but a contributing part, a fraction, of the world's one great ocean. One ocean. The Atlantic, the Indian, the Arctic, the Pacific, the Southern—all connected by waterways and by the currents of the air. And this one ocean breathes life into our shared existence, with the waves marching up and down the coasts, messengers of the magnificent flow of energy from sea to shore. These are facts. I know them to be facts. Yet who could believe it? One ocean, one life, observable from every vantage point on earth, even from my three-windowed wall.

✦

If you must, if you feel it absolutely necessary— for your safety, that is; for your general well-being; or for the sake of your poor old mother (bless her)—shut your eyes. For my part, I shall keep my eyes wide open, like Wittgenstein's. You know Wittgenstein? He called himself an eye in the socket of the world. Wide open. I mean, wide. Even snails blink. But I shall be an eye in the socket of the world so as to detect the pebbles embedded in the quays, the grains of God knows what in the making of a mirror, and every gesture of the heart or head, no matter how invisible to the snail's naked eye, that you, of all people, care to make. See that? The tawny stones in Athens and Jerusalem? See that? Of course you don't. Your eyes are shut tighter than a newborn snail's. Over the shadowy steppes, you traipse like a clodhopper. Are you blind? Am I blind? It is possible that I am blind, even though my eyes are open to everything—the endless sky, everything. This rite of adoration, this seeing, the visible moon in the palm of one's eyes.

✦

I go wandering at the drop of a hat. Whenever a teacher or school official needs someone to volunteer to run an errand uptown—a pickup or delivery—I jump at the chance. It's a win-win situation. I get out of the school, and the school gets rid of me. Uptown can mean anything from Fortieth Street to Ninetieth—any place north of the insistent airless charm of Gramercy Park. Uptown is the city of the established. Men and women in hats, blue serge suits, and crisp, pleated dresses stride boldly this way and that. I love walking among them, the invisible boy in the world of grown-ups who know what side is up and keep their shirts on, and their heads on straight, and their noses clean; go-getters who snap to it, who are right as rain, fit as a fiddle, on the ball, on the money, in the pink; take-charge people who straighten up and fly right and are cooking with gas. I am a Martian in their midst. Do I want to be them someday? In a pig's eye.

Making my way around the city, I sometimes think I am sleepwalking, because of my dreams. Sometimes not. When I'm certain I am dreaming, it turns out I am not. Occasionally, I dream within a dream. Have you done that? It's disorienting. You awaken from the dream within your dream only to find yourself in the first dream, where you are afraid of going to sleep lest you return to your dream inside the original. That inner dream is the one you never remember, the secret dream. It frightens you the most, but maybe it shouldn't. The dream tells you what it wants you to know.

✦

Chuang Tzu, the Taoist philosopher, wondered if he was a man dreaming about a butterfly or a butterfly dreaming about a man. T. S. Eliot said there is just so much reality one can take. I never watch the news, but I believe in dreams. The early Greeks did too. They believed in the power of dreams so devotedly, they saw themselves as living in two worlds simultaneously. Dual citizenship. Count me in.

Everyone lives in dreams, at least part of the time, especially when one is dimly aware of a former life. Déjà vu and all that. Cavafy wrote of the Poseidonians who, centuries after being conquered by the Tyrrhenians and waves of other marauders, forgot the Greek language they were born with. Forgot their native tongue. Poof. All of them.

What must it be like to be something and then to forget the something you were? Whoever you were originally murmurs in the fluted columns of your heart. You were Greek, but no one knows it, including yourself. Every so often you blurt out a word in Greek, but you don't know why, and you don't know what the word means.

The thing about dreams is that they exist in three tenses at once. Some things one recalls from dreams simply haven't happened yet, and they may never happen. You may forget them. Other things are worth holding on to. Your hand, for instance.

✦

Whatever happened to Stewart Granger? And Jane Greer? And Gloria DeHaven? And Joan Blondell? Whatever happened to Joan Blondell? Do these people just appear, then vanish forever? Is that what the world will do? Appear for a while, then be gone as though it were never here? I receive daily bulletins about George Clooney, Kanye West, and Miley Cyrus. Why doesn't someone tell me about Pat O'Brien? Whatever happened to Pat O'Brien? Or Willie Best? Or Keye Luke? There ought to be a Missing Persons Bureau for such missing persons. Missing persons are not supposed to be. If there were such a bureau, I'd file plenty of reports, you betcha. Whatever happened to Hattie McDaniel?

Whatever happened to my socks? My passport? Is

everything missing? It is the poems you have lost or the poems William Empson lost. Whatever happened to William Empson? Or to Kurt Weill and Maxwell Anderson after they wrote "September Song"? I think I'll look in the lost and found. Whatever happened to the lost and found?

While we're at it, whatever happened to *you*? You were here a minute ago. There is life before death. Whatever happened to you?

✦

A distant cousin of mine, whom I never met, survived Auschwitz. He had been a lawyer and legal scholar in Germany before the Nazis seized the country. When the war was over, and the extermination camps were liberated, my cousin came here and settled in Brockton, Massachusetts, where he found a job selling shoes in a shoe store. He was by then in his sixties. After a few months, the owner of the store approached my cousin and told him that he would like to promote him to assistant manager. Clearly, my cousin was too well educated and had too distinguished a bearing for a mere sales job. My cousin thanked the owner but said he would prefer to have no higher position than the one he held. He was content to sell shoes to people who came to the store because they needed shoes.

The world is a refugee. The world is a dream within a dream. The world is a yogurt, no, a culvert, no, a yogurt; the world is a killer from the egg. The world is a defeated brigade, dragging around a corner, bandaged from head to toe, with a wound in its snare drum. The world drums. The world dreams. The world sings the old standards, like "September Song." The world sings off key, sharp and flat. The world sinks in the moraine of poetry, weeping, never to surface. The world is a selkie. The world is Kaddish. The world is kiddish. The world is skittish. The world is the sea in winter. The world is not the sea in winter. The world is small beer. The world is a bier. A small bier in Sudan. The world is a light in silence and, then again, not. The world imagines you as you imagine it. The world speaks your language. The world speaks no language, certainly not yours or that of the Greeks. The world is a meal made out of nettles. The world nettles. The world starves, save on those occasions when, gluttonous to the gills, it swallows the Elgin Marbles and nibbles on its own red thumb. The world. What may one say about the world? The world is Cadafy and Conquest. The world is not Cadafy and Conquest. No way is the world Cadafy and Conquest. You can count on that, by gum. The world is a cathedral-shaped clock clacking in the maple-walled entrance hall of a great dark manse, deserted by the servants, on a high hill where it rained only this morning and where calves and bibliophiles graze. The world is a repeat offender. You are the world. Have a Coke? The world is Thomas Carlyle's fireplace and Chuang Tzu's butterfly. The world is no such thing.

✦

In life as in love, wait and see. I'm thinking of Betty, a woman in her sixties who came to the homeless shelter only a few months before she died. Betty sang for coins on Broadway—the standards, in her cigarette rasp. Yet one could tell a voice had been there once. In spite of having endured shock therapy at several mental hospitals, as well as a long life on the streets, she still showed the apple cheeks of a girl.

My friend Garry and I produced a journal in the shelter, in which we interviewed the clients and wrote their stories. The journal was a private enterprise, meant only for the people in the shelter. The profiles, we found, helped to certify their lives. So I asked Betty if she would mind being interviewed. "If I have the time, Roger," she said. "But you know how it is. I have my regular gig at the Latin Quarter.

And then Hollywood is supposed to call any any day now to set up my screen test. That's what happens when you're crowned Miss America."

I asked the psychiatrist connected with the shelter if there would be any harm in writing Betty's story, even though it seemed wholly implausible. "Not if she believes it," he said. So dutifully I wrote it all down, as Betty told it. Then, out of curiosity, I decided to find out if there was anything to her story. There was a lot to it. She had not been Miss America, though she had been runner-up in the Miss Cincinnati beauty pageant. She had risen to fame in the city as a singer at the Latin Quarter. She had had a Hollywood screen test. In an old *Life* magazine, I came across a picture of Betty dancing with Joe DiMaggio.

Something terrible must have happened to her after the screen test, some sort of breakdown, because the next anyone knew of her, Betty was a patient in a Baltimore mental hospital. There she was raped by an attendant and gave birth to a girl. The baby was given away. Betty was shuttled among more hospitals, including New York's Bellevue. Eventually, she landed her final gig, singing for handouts on upper Broadway, in front of Weber's Closeout Center, where sweaters went for seven cents.

Two weeks before Betty died, her daughter,

Lee, now in her twenties, who had spent a lifetime searching for her mother, found Betty in the shelter. She was introduced to her mother as a visitor who had come a long way. "How ya doin'?" Betty greeted her daughter, whom she seemed to know at once— same round face, same short hair, same slant of the eyebrows and apple cheeks. At Betty's memorial service, they played a recording of what she used to call her bebop version of "What a Friend We Have in Jesus." A few old pals from the Latin Quarter sang along. First you wait, then you see.

✦

A man in town found a message lying on the beach. The ink was soaked from seawater, but the note was nonetheless legible. All it said was, "If you receive this message, call the following number as soon as possible." It was signed "Forrest Shackleton, age 12," and dated November 19, 1974. The man who'd found the note brought it to the other villagers, who gathered round, each reading the message and mulling it over. "Do you think we should call the number?" they asked. The note had been written forty-five years earlier. No one even recognized the area code. Sure enough, when they tried the number on the note, it had long been disconnected. When they tried to Google Forrest Shackleton, nothing came up. Do you suppose Forrest just tossed the note in the ocean on a whim, or did he really need help? That was what troubled the villagers. The thought that a little boy had been in danger, even forty-five years in the past, worried and saddened them. They felt somehow that they had failed him. For days after that, the people spoke of little other than Forrest. Had he been threatened all those years ago, and was he all right now? Had he found safety and happiness even though no one had answered his note? How helpless and useless one feels when one cannot reach a fellow creature across time and space.

✦

One August evening, my dad, a doctor who specialized in diseases of the lungs, was waiting for a train at the East Hampton railroad station. Two young men were approaching the station in a white convertible just as the train was pulling in. Instead of stopping at the warning sign, they sped up in order to cross the tracks ahead of the train. The convertible spun its wheels and stalled. The locomotive hit it head on, crushing the car and pinning the young men to the dashboard.

My father joined others rushing to the site of the crash. The men in the car were within minutes of dying. The only thing my father could do was to give them morphine to try to reduce the pain. He told me this later, with a look of sorrowful helplessness—the same look I'd seen on his face when talking of his terminal lung-cancer patients.

There's some question as to whether the men actually did feel pain at the moment of their dying. A hypothesis suggests that at the moment of death, peptide hormones are released by cells in the hypothalamus and pituitary gland. Endorphins. They attach themselves to the cells responsible for feeling pain.

Lewis Thomas, the physician, biologist, and author of the admired *The Lives of a Cell*, told me that when he was in the army in Okinawa, he saw two MPs drive their jeep into a tank. The jeep was crushed flat. As people worked like crazy to pry the MPs from the wreckage, the two men chatted as if nothing had happened, even apologizing for the accident. Then they died. Lewis felt that such events proved the basic kindness of nature.

I'm sure my father was not thinking of endorphins or of the kindness of nature when he gave morphine to the men at the railroad station. He simply did what he could to reduce their agony. Then he walked away, dumb struck and stooped under the weight of his inability to save two lives. This helplessness to rescue others. There is no pain like it in the world.

✦

Questions for the late, great Stephen Hawking:

Who created the universe?
Who created the creator?
If God created the universe, how much of a free hand
    did he or she have—as a creator, I mean?
Does God have hands?
Is the universe a compendium of equations, like that
    $E=MC^2$ business?
Does the universe have a purpose?
Does everything have a purpose?
Can the act of thinking accomplish everything?
You posited that the universe can come to an end.
    What shall we do till then?

✦

I advise you to hold hands as you walk,
And speak not a word.
    —ROBERT PENN WARREN, "August Moon"

✦

If I were asked to create God—from scratch, I mean,
the way Thomas Carlyle rewrote his history—I'd
start with an ocean wave and build from there. One
wave would become several, then several billion, and

the power and the glory would finally reveal itself in the cold comfort of the noncommittal, calm, and exploding sea. My kind of God.

✦

When I am fifteen, a view of the universe seems to be taking hold. It grows in part from Betty, and from the weeping girl in Columbus Circle, and also from the bearded lady in Coney Island—from the observable truth that everyone bears a burden of one sort or another and that everyone is lonely bearing that burden. Add that thought to the fact that everybody dies, and you come to the conclusion that there are two sure things, not one, connected with being human: death and loneliness. Everyone is lonely and everyone dies. What I gain from arriving at this idea I am not sure. Confidence, maybe. The confidence of definition and clarity. I am on my own in the world, and the world is on its own in the universe. And if loneliness and death are the two givens of human existence, the acknowledgment of both must be necessary for living, however incoherent life may seem. We will die and we are lonely. We live in one another's shadow.

✦

The trick to survival is not to believe in the things that threaten it. To turn a willful blind eye to the evidence. If, for instance, I were to leave my station by the three-windowed wall and go down to the beach and see a wave begin to form in the middle distance and rise up in the shape of a black alp, until it was so vast, it blotted out the Cold Moon and the stars, and it started progressing toward me, definite and irrefutable, I would ignore it. Sit on the cold sand, stare straight at it, and ignore it. I would tell myself that the wave was a fiction. That I was imagining it. And soon, I would imagine it gone.

The techniques of catharsis are magical, not rational. If one believes in the perpetual relocation of the soul, it follows that the soul is older than any body it inhabits. We carry the past inside us as if it were an extra bone. People say of quiet and wise young people that they have an "old soul." Everyone does.

What then is the relationship of body and soul or the effect of the soul on the body? Is the body merely a carrier? Are we all surrogate mothers? Or is the body, the soul's container, the more magical entity in that it actually and demonstrably lives— in the future, for the future, without, of course, knowing the future. The transmigrating soul need

not concern itself with life in the future. It is a perpetual denizen of the past. The body, in contrast,
walks forward.

✦

Brown kettle; kelp; life; a cracked jug of water; a
kid slapped in Central Park; a wave from an office
window; life; a tidal wave; the irrevocable water;
on the Cape, the declension of the tides; some joint
you've got here; Bill Evans plays "Like Someone in
Love"; save the boys in Thailand; cave (cavern), cave
(beware); grab the oar; scrub the crockery; mind
the sand martins; mind the martinis; mind the ice
cubes from Antarctica; mind your manners; mind
the store; who here's from Queens?; but see what
you've done with the water; pigs shy away from the
colters; life; coralline filaments on the reefs; every
artery of the river screams bloody murder; every
cone of water; it's water, Ma, just water; and Jimmy
Joyce's moocow; and "a strange light glowing faintly
upon her frail flesh"; her frail, liquid flesh; self-bap-
tized, chalky flesh; lick the salt off her hands; sea
grass and seaweed and seaward leeward, on the
night of the Cold Moon; splash and silence; "It was
so whimsical"; a night at the Latin Quarter; life; a
freeze; a frieze; grab hold of the pieces; there must
be a stalactite here somewhere; if only one knew its

dialect; if only one knew the terrain; the subterrane, for the boys in Thailand; go fish; water and daughter; water pouring over white bones in the dark; life; I am more chaff than wheat; clay is the word, and clay is the flesh; the moon's in shreds.

✦

I am seven, riding my bike in Weston, Connecticut, where my parents have taken a farmhouse for the summer in what is then a rural village. My mother is with my one-year-old brother. My father is in the city. The day is very hot, and I am sweating yet moving fast through the heavy air. I always go fast. I make up bike races in my head and win every one. I come from behind, catch up to the leaders, then shoot ahead.

On a road I have not taken before, I ride over a stump of a hill and come upon a group of kids in what look like Boy Scout uniforms. They are taking turns shooting arrows at a huge red-and-white archery target on a tripod. All the archers are very good. They must be ten- or twelve-year-olds. One after the other, they shoot three arrows apiece. Several of the kids pierce the bull's-eye, yet they do not celebrate or congratulate one another. They take this archery practice very seriously, like ancient warriors preparing for battle.

Straddling my seat on the bike, I lower the kick-stand and watch the bigger kids for a long time. I say nothing to them, and they do not appear to notice me. It all seems strange—this determined archery practice in the middle of a hot summer day, in the middle of nowhere. The leaves on the trees are stock still.

A young man dressed in a scoutmaster uniform has been scrutinizing the archers. He retrieves an errant arrow, looks up and sees me. He appears anxious, fretful, as he approaches. "Are you supposed to be here?" he says. I tell him, "I don't know."

✦

Are you familiar with Zeno's paradox? That if you shoot an arrow at a target, the arrow will travel half the distance to the target, then half the remaining distance, then half that, and so on, to infinity, never to hit the target it flies toward? But, of course, the arrow does hit the target—thus the paradox. This problem is supposed to show how manipulatable reality is.

But I see Zeno's paradox rather as a test of will. If you were the arrow in question and simply wanted to loiter around in space, you could persuade yourself that you will never hit the target and live satisfied with dissatisfaction ever after. You could progress in an eternity of halves.

Instead, I suggest that this stalling is all word-play. If you have the right bow and arrow and the right target, you can go anywhere. Anywhere.

✦

Come do it, while you can. Come help them. They do not call you. They do not know you. But come help anyway. In a shiver of wild flowers, in the seepage of the December ocean, as a cortege of blackbirds passes by—do it. No need to be territorial. Extend the borders of your authority to the ferrymen, the nervous Nellies, the tailors, the traitors, the birders, the hoi polloi. In a snit, in a rage, in a snow-storm—the sea white as a sheet of paper—make a mad dash for them before the gates slam shut. You still have time. He who hesitates is toast. Those tanks? The machine guns mounted on the tripods? They can't hit the side of a barn. Under the board-walk, fish slap themselves to death. Pack up your commas and your consonants. Unfortunately, the brass band is on holiday at the Ritz, so you'll have to come unheralded. Don't worry. Nothin' to it. No preparation necessary. You look fine. (Oh, this old thing?) And lose the fruit basket. Come as you are.

✦

First light. I drift amid the flotsam like bait, circling the traps. I paddle on my back, playing otter, cracking clamshells with my paws. In a passing gondola, a radio plays on the nodes of the blues. Ten-thousand-year-old bones of a murdered tribe rise up in Kenya and reassemble themselves. We are all repeat offenders. One day, I'll go out and douse the flamethrowers, sink the armadas, and play seven-string guitar for schoolchildren. One day I'll comb the beach for bottles containing notes from the past. One day I'll die.

But not today. Today, I play "September Song" on the piano. Today the wind ruffles the fretted terrain of Mars. The mimosa grows in Brooklyn. The stairway climbs to heaven, where love is. The selkies sleep. The eggs hatch. The cells chat, "We are life. We are love. And we are responsible for each other." I troll my paw in the water and feel candles.

And these few precious days I'll spend with you. These precious days I'll spend with you.

About the Author

ROGER ROSENBLATT is the author of five *New York Times* Notable Books of the Year, four national bestsellers, and seven off-Broadway plays. His essays for *Time* magazine and the *PBS NewsHour* have won two George Polk Awards, the Peabody, and the Emmy, among others. In 2015, he won the Kenyon Review Award for Lifetime Literary Achievement. He held the Briggs-Copeland appointment in the teaching of writing at Harvard. He is Distinguished Professor of English and Writing and SUNY Stony Brook/Southampton.